Propensity for Violence

By

Lawrence Hutton

A Propensity for Violence

All rights reserved.

Copyrights © 2023

Author: Lawrence Hutton

ISBN: 979-8-218-14905-5

Table of Contents

The Violence on Native Americans	Pg. 5
The Violence on African Americans	Pg. 12
The Violence of White Supremacy	Pg. 33
The Violence of White Supremacy in Religion	Pg. 51
A need to be Superior	Pg. 57
The Propensity for Violence	Pg. 70

Preface

In the spring of May 19th, 1918, in Brooks County Georgia, a Mob of white men lynched an 8th month pregnant Mary Turner. Simply for speaking against the lynching of her husband the day before. As they lynched her, they tied her feet and proceeded to hang her upside down and then poured gasoline on her and set her a fire. Sadly, she did not die right away. As she hung there burning one of the men took a butcher knife and cut the baby from her stomach and as the crying baby fell to the ground one of the members of the mob crushed the baby's head with his foot. And if that were not enough the lynch mob fired over one hundred bullets into her body. All stemming from her Husband being alleged to have killed a white farmer. This story most of all was the motivation to write this book. To not just read how a black man was killed i.e., Martin Luther King. Or as Emmett Till.

Yes, murder is murder, and no murder is right or justified, but to know that you not only lynched, and burned a pregnant woman, but you cut her unborn child from her stomach and killed it the minute it hit the ground. This country and its western culture have a history of violence against people of colors and religion. This country has a **"Propensity for Violence."**

The Violence on Native Americans

Since the arrival of Colonist to North America there has been violence and genocide originally directed toward the American Indians, The original Americans. If it were not for the original Americans, the colonist would have died. They had no idea about hunting, planting etc. Native Americans lived in peace and where able to be one with nature, but Colonist brought violence to Native America the whole premise of scalping to the Native Americans, Colonist, who also used scalping as a means to collect bounty. In the beginning there was a bounty for every dead Indian. Just claim you killed so many Indians, then one had to bring the heads of the Indian but that became too cumbersome, so the other option was to take the scalp which was easy to carry in a bag. So, it was so many dollars for every scalp shown. This Nation was born in violence and its embrace of the doctrine that they were the original Americans, and the Indians were the inferior race.

Propensity for Violence

History shows that Western Culture time and again has no problem in the eradication of any race other than their own, call it what you like, massacre genocide it all ends with the same results. The Western Culture has become a void of violence and racial superiority. The need to rule and have domain overall. This while most Nations have learned to live in peace sharing each other's cultures time and again.

Case in point, in the state of Maryland there is a region known on the map as Route 210, also known as Indian Head Highway that runs from the District of Columbia to Charles County. Legend has it that RT210 was a foot path colonist marked the trail with the heads of the Piscataway Indian Tribe on sticks and then their scalps. To just kill a young Indian Warrior and cut the scalp from his head and not even blink just for the money or trophy. How easy it is to kill, butcher, rape, burn, and mutilate a human being. How the Native American Indian had to deal with genocide by the American Government and American Settlers who walked onto Indian Reservations and ripped the children from the arms of American Indian Mothers. Between the sixteen states 85% of those children were removed from the home and placed into Foster Care or placed into homes of American Settlers. In 1879 Colonist Carlisle Indian Industrial School, dedicated to "Kill the Indian, save the Man." Was opened. Its aim was to forced native children to assimilate Western Culture. They were not allowed to speak their own language or practice their own religion. They were also subject to physically and sexually abuse at the hands of their care givers. In 1929 the Navajo Children were placed in Government run Boarding Schools to, what they called *"Civilize them."*

Propensity for Violence

From the moment Western Culture and Native Americans met, the West felt the need to conquer this American Frontier to kill and or conquer the Native American Indian. They felt that they were superior to them for whatever reason, and realized. I can take what they have, all I have to do is kill all the men of fighting age, take their land and their women because it is my destiny and Gods will, and that's what Western Culture did. So the battle began, arrow against gun, canon against spear, massacre after massacre. As the bodies of Young Warriors lay dead on the battlefield. As the story goes that American Pioneers and Settlers were able to fend off the savages.

Propensity for Violence

As written in American History, Settlers survived the cross country trek, battling starvation sickness and yes the savage Indians. The same savages who Settlers slaughtered, scalped, and took land from them and placed them on reservations, their children taken from them and placed into a Foster Homes, where their children were made to assimilate western lifestyle and repeatedly sexually assault by the operators and staff. The sad fact when you look at what and how western culture does things regarding the eradication of any race of color. By either straight slaughter or culture and or religions eradication by assimilation. They killed those who they knew would fight or who would be a threat and those who are left would be made to conform to western culture and religion.

Native American Indian Massacres

The Gnadenhutten Massacre: In 1782, a group of militiamen from Pennsylvania killed 96 Christianized Delaware Indians, illustrating the growing contempt for native people. Captain David Williamson ordered the converted Delaware, who had been blamed for attacks on white settlements, to go to the cooper shop two at a time, where militiamen beat them to death with wooden mallets and hatchets.

The Creek War: In the South, the War of 1812 bled into the Mvskoke Creek War of 1813-1814, also known as the Red Stick War. An inter-tribal conflict among Creeks Indian factions, the war also engaged U.S. militias, along with the British and Spanish, who backed the Indians to help keep Americans from encroaching on their interests. Early Creek victories inspired General Andrew Jackson to retaliate with 2,500 men, mostly Tennessee militia, in early November 1814. To avenge the Creek led massacre at Fort Mims, Jackson and his men slaughtered 186 Creeks at Tallushatchee. "We shot them like dogs!" said Davy Crockett.

Propensity for Violence

Forced Removal: In his annual address to Congress in 1833, Jackson denounced Indians, stating, "They have neither the intelligence, the industry, the moral habits, nor the desire of improvement which are essential to any favorable change in their condition. Established during another and a superior race…they must necessarily yield to the force of circumstances and ere [before] long disappear. "From 1830 to 1840, the U.S. army removed 60,000 Indians Choctaw, Creek, Cherokee and others— from the East in exchange for additional territory west of the Mississippi. Thousands died along the way of what became known as the "Trail of Tears." And as whites pushed ever westward, the Indian-designated territory continued to shrink.

The Sand Creek Massacre: Indians fighting back to defend their people and protect their homelands provided ample justification for American forces to kill *any* Indians on the frontier, even peaceful ones. On November 29, 1864, a former Methodist minister,

Propensity for Violence

John Chivington, led a surprise attack on peaceful Cheyenne's and Arapahos on their reservation at Sand Creek in southeastern Colorado. His force consisted of seven hundred men, volunteers in the First and Third Colorado Regiments. Plied with too much liquor the night before, Chivington and his men boasted that they were going to kill Indians.

Once a missionary to Wyandot Indians in Kansas, Chivington declared, "Damn any man who sympathizes with Indians! I have come to kill Indians, and believe it is right and honorable to use any means under God's heavens to kill Indians. "That fateful cold morning, Chivington led his men against 200 Cheyenne's and Arapahos. Cheyenne Chief Black Kettle had tied an American flag to his lodge pole as he was instructed, to indicate his village was at peace. When Chivington ordered the attack, Black Kettle tied a white flag beneath the American flag, calling to his people that the soldiers would not kill them. As many as 160 were massacred, mostly women and children.

Custer's Campaigns: At this time, a war hero from the Civil War emerged in the West. George Armstrong Custer rode in front of his mostly Irish Seventh Cavalry to the Irish drinking tune, "Gary Owen." Custer wanted fame and killing Indians— especially peaceful ones who were not expecting to be attacked—represented opportunity. On orders from General Philip Sheridan, Custer and his Seventh attacked the Cheyenne's and their Arapaho allies on the western frontier of Indian Territory on November 29, 1868, near the Washita River. After slaughtering 103 warriors, plus women and children, Custer dispatched to Sheridan that "a great victory was won," and described, "One, the Indians were asleep. Two, the women and children offered little resistance. Three, the Indians are bewildered by our change of policy." Custer later led the Seventh Cavalry on the northern Plains against the Lakota, Arapahos, and Northern Cheyenne's. He boasted, "The Seventh can manage anything it meets," and "there are not enough Indians in the world to defeat the Seventh Cavalry. "Expecting another great surprise.

victory, Custer attacked the largest gathering of warriors on the high plains on June 25, 1876—near Montana's Little Big Horn River. Custer's death at the hands of Indians making their own last stand only intensified propaganda for military revenge to bring "peace" to the frontier.

Wounded Knee: Anti-Indian anger rose in the late 1880s as the Ghost Dance spiritual movement emerged, spreading to two dozen tribes across sixteen states, and threatening efforts to culturally assimilate tribal peoples. Ghost Dance, which taught that Indians had been defeated and confined to reservations because they had angered the gods by abandoning their traditional customs, called for a rejection of the white man's ways.

Propensity for Violence

In December 1890, several weeks after the famed Sioux Chief Sitting Bull was killed while being arrested, the U.S. Army's Seventh Cavalry massacred 150 to 200 ghost dancers at Wounded Knee, South Dakota, for their mass murder of disarmed Lakota, President Benjamin Harrison awarded about 20 soldiers the Medal of Honor. And now we have come to the point in History where Western Culture has won. They have conquered the Native American and not only fought and defeated their Warriors, but erased and killed their culture, their religion, and their whole way of life. Totally erased it from History on a placed of a piece of land. While the tribal lands they once owned and hunted on are now homes, hotels, highways, and casinos.

Violence on African Americans

In the continent of African families and tribes lived in mostly peace and harmony. Men took their sons out into the jungle to teach them how to hunt and learn how to fight and protect if called upon. Mothers took their daughters out to the fields to learn how to forage, make clothing, cook and how to be a Wife to their future Husband and Mother to their future Children, and all knew how to respect nature and the land. Everyone knew their place in the grand scheme of things. All was well until the day when ship after ship came and snatched Africans from their land. They were literality kidnaped from their homeland, brought here in chains, and beaten into submission. And there again the Western Cultures need to be superior to another race, western culture also employed religion into their propensity for violence. Prior to the civil war whites owned slaves we all know, they tried to justify economic exploitation of Black people by creating a scientific theory of white superiority and Black inferiority. In 1785 The then President Thomas Jefferson wrote about the inferiority of blacks to white.

Propensity for Violence

The civil war upheld the need for state secession and creation of a confederate state in America. In 1890, author **L. Frank Baum** wrote:

The whites by law of conquest, by justice of civilization, are masters of the American Continent, and the best safety of the frontier settlements will be secured by the total annihilation of the few remaining Indians.

Make no mistake about it, the mere existence of White Supremacy is a justification for White Violence against those of color. It is odd how Western Culture stereo types other countries, and cultures as savages, third world. The American Indian in their history books and Western Movies where labeled as pure savages and primitives that needed to be eradicated. Africans were labeled as savages and primitives, and still are.

These primitives were brought out of the dark ages and given Christianity by Anglo-Saxon Protestants. There were moments in American History where some proclaimed Anglo-Saxon Christians acted as the ultimate savage.

One: Women Slaves

The worst combination was to be a slave and a woman. Female slaves were never safe from perverted masters. Masters would subject female slaves to many sexual savageries. They took turns with their sons and relatives to violate them.

Propensity for Violence

Two: Men Slaves

Male slaves were not safe from abuse by their masters and their sons. Some male slaves were purchased by their owners solely by the size of their penis. And they were often raped by their gay slave owners. This process is called ***breaking the buck***.

Three: Forced Castration

According to Historian Dr. E Franklin Frazier, male slaves were also forced to indulge in sex with female slaves. But they were weighed and physically tested before they were placed in a room with young women to mate and reproduce strong babies. Allegedly, if they could not bear children, their testicles were castrated.

Four: Forced Pregnancies

The mortality rate among slaves was extremely high. So, owners often forced female slaves to have children even at the age of thirteen. It was an obligation for female slaves to begin bearing children at this very young age to replenish the slave stock. They were expected to have four or five children by the age of twenty. And if female slaves could live up to that expectation, there was a "promise" that they could be granted freedom.

Five: Baby Makers

Likewise, male slaves were expected to start fathering children at the age of fifteen. They were first inspected to see if they could breed well. Young male slaves were expected to get at least 12 female slaves pregnant in a period of 5 years. And according to narratives from slaves, a particular male slave by the name of Bert managed to father over 200 children during his lifetime.

Six: Punishments

Female slaves who did not cooperate with their owners to bear children for them were subjected to many and various punishments. These included mental torture like separation from her family. Torture could also be inflicted physically. If a female slave did not or could not bear children, the result was harsh working conditions. She was not given any breaks or rewards that were given to mothers. And she would do the same work on the level of men.

Seven: Privileges

Female slaves who obliged and bore children for their owners were offered a lot of privileges. These included gifts, for instance, extra clothing, no more harsh treatments, and sometimes freedom.

Eight: Forced Divorces

Slave owners would sometimes split up married couples and require them to choose new partners. And a slave wife could never be faithful to her husband. Most slave owner demanded that married slave women should have affairs with other men.

Nine: Beheading

If a female slave was very pretty, it meant they would get better treatment than the rest. Pretty female slaves often worked inside the house. But the slave owners' wives often got jealous at the affection and favor that their husbands showed female slaves. Hence, the slave owners' wives beheaded any children bore from pretty female slaves.

Ten: Sexual Entertainment

The masters would arrange orgies ("*a wild party characterized by excessive drinking and indiscriminate sexual activity*") among the slaves. This was a way to provide entertainment for the masters' friends. And the friends could join in the orgies if they desired.

Eleven: Incest

Whilst some owners abandoned the children they fathered with female slaves, not all did. Some gave their offspring education and money. But some kept the children for their own sick benefits. They went on to father more children with their daughters and indulge in sex with their sons.

Propensity for Violence

Lynching first started around 1890, at that time only whites were the victims of this act, normally means to kill or hang someone. Between 1862 and 1968 70% of the victims of lynching where African Americans. There was also no sexual discrimination on lynching. African American Men and Women where lynched.

United States Supreme Court's rulings in cases like *The Slaughterhouse Cases*, 83 U.S. 36 (1872); *United States v. Reese*, 92 U.S. 214 (1875); and *United States v. Cruikshank*, 92 U.S. 542 (1876).

And without fail Western Culture also place Black children in Boarding School as they did the Native American Indians with the same results. This was also the beginning of the Juvenile Justice System. And like the current system the Juveniles Facility was getting $12.50 a month for boarding these Black children and while using these children as free labor. After the 13th Amendment Western Culture had a hard time standing side by side with their once Private Property and be made to be treated their equal so that might be a hard pill to swallow. The hate ran so deep that African Americans were killed simply for refusing to do what a white man said or if they talked back. That also caused the rise in lynching and killing by either shooting or bombing areas were African Americans lived, we currently called it **Terrorism.** So called freed slaves where still not free. Yes, we were free…. on paper, but we were never free. To this day we still are not free. You see there is a catch in the 13th Amendment and here is the part where it is a problem for the African American…

Propensity for Violence

On February 1, 1865, President Abraham Lincoln approved the Joint Resolution of Congress submitting the proposed amendment to the state legislatures. The necessary number of states (three-fourths) ratified it by December 6, 1865. The 13th Amendment to the United States Constitution provides that

"Neither slavery nor involuntary servitude, except as a punishment for crime whereof the party shall have been duly convicted, shall exist within the United States, nor any place subject to their jurisdiction."

"Except," this is the part where it becomes a problem. Not only where there Criminal Laws on the books the freed Black people could be charged with but Jim Crow Laws as well that when used against use would put us into the Criminal Justice System and right back into slavery.

Also in the letter of the law was the justification to kill Black people. More so on just be accused then being proven. All one had to say was a black man killed a white man and his fate was sealed. Yes there was a trial, but that was just the criminal justice system going through the motions. Everyone knew at the end of the trail the black man was going to be found guilty and he was going to be execute. Even in cases where there was an allegation by a white woman of rape. That was punishable by death. There has been story after story. I know of one story in particular where a white man would leave his wife to meet with a Black woman for sex. So the wife found a black man who she would have come over to have an affair with her. One night the husband returned home to find his wife having consensual sex with her black lover. The husband beat the black man and forced his wife to tell police that she was raped. During trial, with an all-white jury. Everyone wondered why the Black man never took the stand to testify in his own behave. He knew just as well that one he was black, two she was white, and three no one at that time on God's Green earth would believe him. Even if there was a jury who would believe his story it would still the fact that that a Nigger touched a White Woman and that my friends were forbidden. And yes, he was put to death by hanging that same day. So needless to say that when a white male committed a crime even of murder against an African American more than not because of an all-white jury they would be found not guilty. Not because of a lack of evidence and or witnesses, because there where more than enough cases of white men confessing or solid proof, no white male would send another white male to jail for killing a black. That goes for rape, arson, and the list goes on. Let's look at what happed in Tulsa, an all-black city. Black homeowners,

Black business owners, black bank owners. Then came the all-white lynch mob. Who shot, and burned, and bombed, and killed. And not even one spent any serious time in jail and or prison. No punishment. So, let us look at punishment. If a white was convicted of a crime, at most and even now they are just looking a jail time. It is rare that they might have gotten the death penalty. Even if they were there would be protesters out front the jail asking for a stay of execution. There was a white man on death row in Seattle Washington back in the 90's for a murder of a woman and raping of a little girl. For a week people stood outside the prison demanding a commute of his sentence. But if so much as a black man gets accused they're lucky if it even makes it to the inside of a courtroom.

So, let us look a punishment. As we know there has been several types of punishment.

1) Jail time
2) Life in jail
3) Electric chair
4) Gas Chamber
5) Hanging
6) Lethal Injection
7) Firing Squad

Whippings: In America, slaves, including pregnant women and children, were often whipped as punishment.

Mutilations: Particularly in cases where slaves had fought each other or resisted their owners or overseers, it was common for owners to order bodily mutilation.

Branding: Branding refers to searing the flesh with a heated metal instrument. This type of torture was typically done to denote ownership.

Smoked Alive: A common practice used in Virginia. He described an owner who had his slaves bound and whipped in the smokehouse. Then he created a fire from tobacco stems to suffocate and "smoke" the slaves as further punishment.

The Hogshead: A slaveholder who hammered nails into a hogshead (large barrel) and left the nail points protruding inside. His slaves were stuffed into these barrels and rolled down long, steep hills while the owner and other slaves watched.

Suspended beneath a cooking fire: A favorite punishment was to tie up a slave, suspend him above the ground, and start a fire above him. A fatty piece of pork was cooked by the fire. Then the burning fat dripped onto the bare skin of the slave.[6]

Demotion or Sale: Many slaves who worked in less physically demanding conditions, such as in the house or in a skilled trade, could be demoted to work in the fields. This resulted in harsher physical conditions, more demanding physical work, and often more violent treatment from owners and overseers.

Public Burning: Many slaves who worked in less physically demanding conditions, such as in the house or in a skilled trade, could be demoted to work in the fields. This resulted in harsher physical conditions, more demanding physical work, and often more violent treatment from owners and overseers.

Long-Term Chaining: In some cases, long lines of slaves were shackled together to perform menial tasks in unison. This was the origin of the chain gangs that became infamous in US prisons.

Forced Reproduction: Following the US Act Prohibiting Importation of Slaves, which became effective in 1808, a shortage of slaves occurred in the South. The internal slave market boomed, which increased the demand for black people. As a result, slaves were often bought and sold based on their "childbearing" capabilities. They were forced to have sex with other slaves to produce more children.

Race of Defendants Executed in the U.S. Since 1976

Race	Number	Percentage
Black	530	34%
Latinx	129	8%
White	861	56%
Other	29	2%

NOTE: The federal government counts some categories, such as Hispanics, as an ethnic group rather than a race. DPIC refers to all groups as races because the sources for much of our information use these categories.

Propensity for Violence

Race of Victims Since 1976

Race	Number	Percentage
Black	353	16%
Latinx	155	7%
White	1699	75%
Other	48	2%

Persons Executed for Interracial Murders in the U.S. Since 1976

Propensity for Violence

"In 82% of the studies [reviewed], race of the victim was found to influence the likelihood of being charged with capital murder or receiving the death penalty, i.e., those who murdered whites were found more likely to be sentenced to death than those who murdered blacks."

– United States General Accounting Office, Death Penalty Sentencing,
February 1990

Race and the Death Penalty

Several studies have shown that race influences the likely hood a defendant will receive the death penalty. In Harris County, Texas, for example, the District Attorney's Office were more than three times as likely to pursue the death penalty against Black defendants than their white counterparts, according to an analysis released in 2013 by University of Maryland criminology professor Ray Paternoster. There is also bias regarding the race of victims in death penalty cases. While Blacks and whites suffer from homicides at about the same rate, the New York Times reports, 80 percent of those executed murdered white people. Such statistics make it easy to understand why African Americans in particular feel that they are not treated fairly by the authorities or in the courts and let us not forget the number of African American Men who were executed but where innocent.

Larry Griffin

Missouri — Convicted: 1981; Executed: 1995

A year-long investigation by the NAACP Legal Defense and Educational Fund has uncovered evidence that Larry Griffin may have been innocent of the crime for which he was executed by the state of Missouri on June 21, 1995. Griffin maintained his innocence until his death, and investigators say his case is the strongest demonstration yet of an execution of an innocent man.

Leo Jones

Florida — Convicted: 1981; Executed: 1998

Jones was convicted of murdering a police officer in Jacksonville, Florida. Jones signed a confession after several hours of police interrogation, but he later claimed the confession was coerced. In the mid-1980s, the policeman who arrested Jones and the detective who took his confession were forced out of uniform for ethical violations. The policeman was later identified by a fellow officer as an "enforcer" who had used torture. Many witnesses came forward pointing to another suspect in the case.

Troy Davis

Georgia — Convicted: 1991; Executed: 2011

After a hearing on September 19, 2011, the **Georgia Board of Pardons and Paroles** denied clemency to **Troy Davis**, despite presentation of testimony casting doubt on his guilt. Brian Kammer, one of Davis's attorneys, said, "I am utterly shocked and disappointed at the failure of our justice system at all levels to correct a miscarriage of justice." Davis's claims of innocence received international attention, and calls for clemency were made by Pope Benedict XVI, former President Jimmy Carter, former FBI Director William Sessions, former Georgia Supreme Court Chief Justice Norman Fletcher and others.

Brian Terrell

Georgia — Convicted: 1995; Executed: 2015

Just before 1:00 a.m. on December 9, 2015, **Georgia** executed **Brian Terrell**. It took a nurse nearly an hour to find a vein for the lethal injection IV and, as the execution drugs were being administered, Terrell mouthed the words: "Didn't do it." His lawyers argued that no physical evidence linked Terrell to the murder and that his conviction and death sentence were the product of prosecutorial misconduct and false and misleading testimony. Physical evidence from the crime scene leaves substantial questions as to Terrell's guilt: footprints found near the victim's body were smaller than Terrell's feet, and none of the 13 fingerprints found by investigators matched his fingerprints. Georgia tried Terrell three times. The first trial ended in a mistrial when jurors could not agree on whether he was guilty. The second resulted in a conviction that was later overturned by the Georgia

Supreme Court. The third trial concluded with a conviction and death sentence.

Domineque Ray

Alabama — Convicted: 1999; Executed: 2019

Alabama executed **Domineque Ray** on February 7, 2019. Ray's execution attracted national attention when Alabama refused to permit his imam to be present in the execution chamber in circumstances in which Christian prisoners were provided religious comfort by a Christian chaplain. However, Ray had also argued that he was innocent and that the evidence against him was false and unreliable. Ray was convicted in July 1999 of the alleged rape, robbery, and murder of 15-year-old Tiffany Harville in Selma, Alabama.

No physical evidence linked Ray to the murder, and the only evidence that Harville had been raped and robbed came from a severely mentally ill man, Marcus Owden, who confessed to the crime and avoided the death penalty by implicating Ray.

Nathaniel Woods
Alabama — Convicted: 2005; Executed: 2020

Nathaniel Woods was sentenced to death after a non-unanimous jury sentencing recommendation in August 2005 for the killings of three **Alabama** police officers. His case featured several hallmarks of wrongful conviction: official misconduct, coerced informant testimony, and racial discrimination. Prosecutors acknowledged that Woods' co-defendant, Kerry Spencer, shot the officers in an incident in a drug house. Spenser, who received a life sentence in his trial, has consistently maintained that he shot the officers in self-defense, after they had beaten Woods during a shakedown and then pointed a gun at Spenser. Knowing he was not the shooter, prosecutors offered Woods a plea deal for 20-25 years, but Woods' lawyer advised him not to take it, misinforming him that he could not be convicted of capital murder as an accomplice.

In the criminal justice system there should be a failsafe to prevent the executions of innocent African Americans. Even as this is being written there are several current court cases involving an African American where Judges are over turning the verdicts and or sentencing and releasing African American men either because it was found that they were truly innocent or they clearly did not have a fair trial. One of the issues I clearly have with the system is where the Prosecution can file a motion to suppress evidence in a case this can what could make an innocent man be found guilty the following will hopefully bring an understanding of what this is.

U.S. Supreme Court

Brady v. Maryland, 373 U.S. 83 (1963)

Brady v. Maryland

No. 490

Argued March 18-19, 1963.

Decided May 13, 1963

373 U.S. 83

Syllabus

In separate trials in a Maryland Court, where the jury is the judge of both the law and the facts, but the court passes on the admissibility of the evidence, petitioner and a companion were convicted of first-degree murder and sentenced to death. At his trial, petitioner admitted participating in the crime, but claimed that his companion did the actual killing. In his summation to the jury, petitioner's counsel conceded that petitioner was guilty of murder in the first degree, and asked only that the jury return that verdict "without capital punishment." Prior to the trial, petitioner's counsel had requested the prosecution to allow him to examine the companion's extrajudicial statements. Several of these were shown to him, but one in which the companion admitted the actual killing was withheld by the prosecution, and did not come to petitioner's notice until after he had been tried, convicted and sentenced, and after his conviction had been affirmed by the Maryland Court of Appeals. In a post-conviction proceeding, the Maryland Court of Appeals held that suppression of the evidence by the prosecutor denied petitioner due process of law, and it remanded the case for a new trial of the question of punishment, but not the question of guilt, since it was of the opinion that nothing in the suppressed confession "could have reduced [petitioner's] offense below murder in the first degree.

"*Held:* Petitioner was not denied a federal constitutional right when his new trial was restricted to the question of punishment, and the judgment is affirmed. Pp. 84-91.

(a) Suppression by the prosecution of evidence favorable to an accused who has requested it violates due process where the evidence is material either to guilt or to punishment, irrespective of the good faith or bad faith of the prosecution. Pp. 86-88.

(b) When the Court of Appeals restricted petitioner's new trial to the question of punishment, it did not deny him due process or equal protection of the laws under the Fourteenth Amendment, since the suppressed evidence was admissible only on the issue of punishment.

Pp. 88-91.226 Md. 422, 174 A.2d 167, affirmed.

So, what does this mean in? The Prosecution can use this just to get a conviction and knowingly send an innocent man to jail. There was a case I will never forget in Kansas, where there were two Black men walking from a bar one night. They came to an intersection and went their separate ways. As the man walk down the dark country road a police cruiser passed by then turns around and stops in front of him. The Trooper gets out, handcuffs him and places him in the back seat. He is driven to a hospital and as the patrol vehicle pulls up front he sees a white woman in a hospital gown sitting in a wheel chair, a doctor on one side and a police detective on the other. The police vehicle slowly drives by and before the man knows it, he's driven straight to jail. So, by the time the smoke cleared, as I always say. He was standing before a Judge being convicted of a Home Invasion and rape and sentence to life. The story of what happened is several black men broke into the woman's home and did rape her.

After his conviction the family was able to obtain a lawyer but sad to say as motion after motion was filed for a retrial on discovery of evidence that the prosecution had suppress during trial 25 years had gone by. His family finally turned to Barry Scheck, a prominent defense attorney who specialized in DNA evidence took his case. Not until Barry Scheck filed the motion for discovery of the DNA evidence did the prosecution for the state of Kansas agreed to release the evidence. But the man had to sign a waiver acknowledging that he would not file a civil suit against the state of Kansas. So, the evidence proved that this man was not even on the scene of the crime, and the state of Kansas knew that, but they wanted a conviction. So unfortunately the man signed after 27 years just to get out of jail for a crime the state of Kansas had Prof He did not do it.

The Violence of White Supremacy

White supremacist

A person who believes that white people constitute a superior race and should therefore dominate society, typically to the exclusion or detriment of other racial and ethnic groups, in particular Black or Jewish people: "an avowed white supremacist."

Supporting the belief that white people constitute a superior race and should therefore dominate society, typically to the exclusion or detriment of other racial and ethnic groups, Black or Jewish.

White supremacy

The belief, theory, or doctrine that white people are inherently superior to people from all other racial and ethnic groups, especially Black people, and are therefore rightfully the dominant group in any society.

White privilege

The unearned and mostly unacknowledged societal advantage that members of the dominant white racial group have, and members of nonwhite groups do not, separate from but compounding with wealth, income, class, education, and other demographic factors that form individual identities:

Propensity for Violence

Pyramid of White Supremacy

Genocide
Mass Murder

Violence
Unjust Police Shootings
Lynching   Hate Crimes

Calls for Violence   Police Brutality
Neo-Nazis   KKK   The N-Word
Confederate Flags   Burning Crosses

Discrimination   Mass Incarceration   Swastikas
Racial Profiling   School-to-prison Pipeline
Hiring Discrimination   Stop and Frisk
Fearing People of Color   Redlining
Racial Slurs   Anti-Immigration Policies
Funding Schools Locally   Predatory Lending

Veiled Racism
Paternalism   Victim Blaming   Racial Jokes
English-only Initiatives   Euro-Centric Curriculum
Racist Mascots   Bootstrap Theory
Tokenism   Cultural Appropriation
Tone Policing   Claiming Reverse Racism   Colorblindness

Minimization   "We all belong to the human race"   Denial of White Privilege
White Savior Complex
"Post-Racial Society"   "Why can't we all just get along?"
"It doesn't matter who you vote for"   White Ally Speaking over POC
"It's just a joke!"   "Get over slavery"   False Equivocation
"Not all white people..."
"But my Black friend said..."   Not Believing Experiences of POC
Prioritizing Intentions over Impact

Indifference
Two Sides to Every Story
"Politics doesn't affect me"   Not Challenging Racist Jokes
Avoiding Confrontation with Racist Family Members   Remaining Apolitical

In a pyramid, every brick depends on the ones below it for support. If the bricks at the bottom are removed, the whole structure comes tumbling down.

Adapted from Ellen Tuzzolo and Safehouse Progressive Alliance for Nonviolence's diagram

White Supremacy goes deeper than just the name used by Western Culture as just a group of insecure white men. I have made the conclusion that it is just what it says. White Supremacy was created just for that, to have total supremacy over everything, economic, social, region, separation from other races. It runs the gambit. In that mix you can also include White Separatism which is a political and social movement that seek separation of white people from other races. This will explain the birth of the original KKK who history just wrote about the lynching and the cross burnings. The original KKK was born December 24, 1865, by six confederate veterans from Tennessee during southern reconstruction using violence which included the Southern Cross in New Orleans and the Knights of the White Camelia in Louisiana. These groups used public violence against black and their allies. If one reads this correctly this sounds the same as what we call todays Domestic Terrorist. As of now the FBI has placed White Supremacist on the list of **Domestic Terrorism**.

Propensity for Violence

(Domestic terrorism or **homegrown terrorism** is a form of terrorism in which victims "within a country are targeted by a perpetrator with the same citizenship" as the victims.)

Some of these **homegrown terrorisms** where:

Dylann Roof   Ted Kaczynski (The Unabomber)

   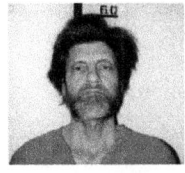

Propensity for Violence

Frank Glenn Miller Jr.   Timothy James McVeigh

These are only four of the many hundreds who have maimed and killed in the name of White Supremacy. Who was that who once said, **"Racism no longer exist in America?"**

Propensity for Violence

White Supremacy has another element that is the power. For decades White American had power over all for the longest and now they see that power slipping from their hands.

"It is not power that corrupts, but fear. Fear of losing power corrupts those who wield it … "

Aung San Suu Kyi

"Power is my mistress. I have worked too hard at her conquest to allow anyone to take her away from me".

Napoleon Bonaparte

White Supremacy in some cases is almost like a religion, and in that religion you have your fanatics. Those who will follow that religion to the letter and whom are also willing to die for that believe. I think that's the difference that separates most other races from the rest. This race will and is willing to die for their cause. That is how strongly they feel about it. This believe is so strong it also carries over into other culture with the same thought processes. I once believed that the hold concept to White Supremacy and the Master Race idea came from Germanys Nazis and Adolph Hitler. But I was wrong. It was the Anglo-Saxon who was the influence to Hitler who accept the idea of Master Race and treating other races especially those races of color to be treated less that human.

Propensity for Violence

We looked at Hitler as evil incarnate. But America was his true inspiration, Hitler observed what Americans were doing to African Americans that even Hitler considered cruel and inhumane by his standards. Hitler looked at how they were treating African Americans and American Indians and adopted the system and called it the Nuremberg Laws.

Nürnberg Laws, two race-based measures depriving Jews of rights, designed by Adolf Hitler and approved by the Nazi Party at a convention in Nürnberg on September 15, 1935. One, the Reichsbürgergesetz (German: "Law of the Reich Citizen"), deprived Jews of German citizenship, designating them "subjects of the state." The other, the Gesetz zum Schutze des Deutschen Blutes und der Deutschen Ehre ("Law for the Protection of German Blood and German Honour"),

usually called simply the Blutschutzgesetz ("Blood Protection Law"), forbade marriage or sexual relations between Jews and "citizens of German or kindred blood." These measures were among the first of the racist Nazi laws that culminated in the Holocaust.

Hitler praised these laws created by the United States. Hitler compared American Negro problem to his Jewish problem but even Nazis saw the future threat "The Negro", posed to the American statesman as the Negro population grew. The German writer Wahrhold Drascher authored, and book titled "Supremacy of the White Race". In that book he was quoted:

"Americans took care to guarantee that the decisive positions in the leadership of the state would be kept in the hands of Anglo-Saxons."

Nazi Germany saw in the 1930's how America had creative policy in government and politics to shape laws that would create a political system base around race. **The Prussian Memorandum** was nothing more that Americas Jim Crow laws. Germany even looked at interracial marriage as **Race Treason**.

By "white supremacy" I do not mean to allude only to the self-conscious racism of white supremacist hate groups. I refer instead to a political, economic, and cultural system in which whites overwhelmingly control power and material resources, conscious and unconscious ideas of white superiority and entitlement are widespread, and relations of white dominance and non-white subordination are daily reenacted across a broad array of institutions and social settings.

Frances Lee Ansley

The targets of hate crime:

In its most recent report, the FBI reported 8,263 against persons, institutions, and property in 2020, compared to 7,314 reported in 2019, a 13% increase and the highest number reported since 2001.

Of the 8,263 hate crimes reported in 2020:

- 2,871 were because of anti-Black bias.
- 1,376 because of sexual orientation or gender identity bias.
- 869 because of anti-white bias.
- 683 because of antisemitic bias.
- 517 because of anti-Hispanic or anti-Latino bias.
- 110 because of anti-Muslim bias.
- 96 because of anti-American Indian or Alaska Native bias.
- 279 because of anti-Asian/Pacific Islander bias.

FBI Hate Crime Statistics for 2020

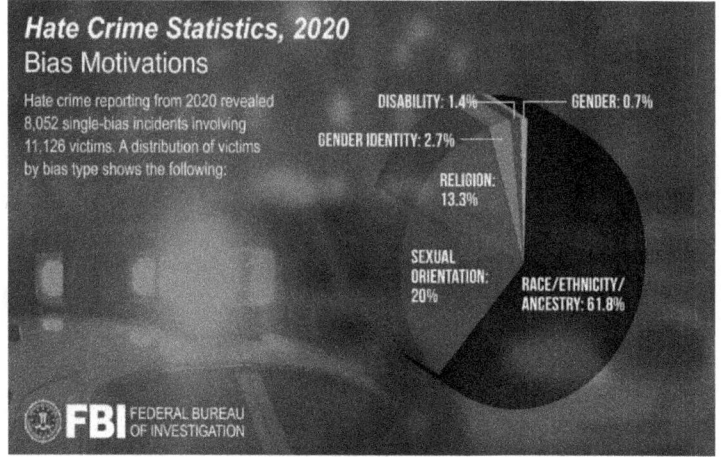

The Department of Justice on Hate Crimes

HATE CRIME LAWS

ABOUT HATE CRIMES

Since 1968, when Congress passed, and President Lyndon Johnson signed into law, the first federal hate crimes statute, the Department of Justice has been enforcing federal hate crimes laws. The 1968 statute made it a crime to use, or threaten to use, force to willfully interfere with any person because of race, color, religion, or national origin and because the person is participating in a federally protected activity, such as public education, employment, jury service, travel, or the enjoyment of public accommodations, or helping another person to do so. In 1968, Congress also made it a crime to use, or threaten to use, force to interfere with housing rights because of the victim's race, color, religion, sex, or national origin; in 1988, protections on the basis of familial status and disability were added. In 1996, Congress passed the Church Arson Prevention Act, 18 U.S.C. § 247.

Under this Act, it is a crime to deface, damage, or destroy religious real property, or interfere with a person's religious practice, in situations affecting interstate commerce. The Act also bars defacing, damaging, or destroying religious property because of the race, color, or ethnicity of persons associated with the property.

In 2009, Congress passed, and President Obama signed, the Matthew Shepard and James Byrd Jr. Hate Crimes Prevention Act, expanding the federal definition of hate crimes, enhancing the legal toolkit available to prosecutors, and increasing the ability of federal law enforcement to support our state and local partners. This law removed then existing jurisdictional obstacles to prosecutions of certain race- and religion-motivated violence, and added new federal protections against crimes based on gender, disability, gender identity, or sexual orientation. Before the Civil Rights Division prosecutes a hate crime, the Attorney General or someone the Attorney General designates must certify, in writing, that (1) the state does not have jurisdiction; (2) the state has requested that the federal government assume jurisdiction; (3) the verdict or sentence obtained pursuant to state charges did not demonstratively vindicate the federal interest in eradicating bias-motivated violence; or (4) a prosecution by the United States is in the public interest and necessary to secure substantial justice.

What is White Privilege?

Particularly white or male privilege is hard to see for those of us who were born with access to power and resources. It is very visible for those to whom privilege was not granted. Furthermore, the subject is extremely difficult to talk about because many white people don't feel powerful or as if they have privileges others do not. It is sort of like asking fish to notice water or birds to discuss air. For those who have privileges based on race or gender or class or physical ability or sexual orientation, or age, it just is- it's normal. The Random House Dictionary (1993) defines privilege as "a right, immunity, or benefit enjoyed only by a person beyond the advantages of most." In her article, "White Privilege and Male Privilege," Peggy McIntosh (1995) reminds us that those of us who are white usually believe that privileges are "conditions of daily experience... [that are] universally available to everybody." Further, she says that what we are really talking about is "unearned power conferred systematically"

African American Massacres

The Fort Pillow Massacre April 12th, 1863,

In response to the Union Army's enlistment of Black men, Confederate President Jefferson Davis promised to execute captured Black troops as slave insurrectionists. White Union troops were taken as prisoners of war, but black ones were to be killed or enslaved. At the Battle of Fort Pillow in Tennessee, Confederates under the command of General Nathan Bedford Forrest fulfilled this order when they slaughtered an estimated 300 surrendering black soldiers, some even as they lay wounded in hospital tents. Two dozen others were castrated.

The New Orleans massacre April 30th, 1866

In 1866, at the Louisiana Constitutional Convention, ex-Confederates led by the Mayor of New Orleans opened fire on a parade of 130 black men celebrating the convention before attacking those in the convention hall. By the time they ran out of ammunition, 238 were dead, the majority of whom were black Union veterans or delegates. Federal troops arrived too late to stop the violence and although the mayor lost his office, no one faced charges for the massacre.

The Colfax Massacre April 13th, 1873

After a contested election in Louisiana, armed, white Democrats and ex-Confederates overpowered Black Republicans who were protecting a courthouse from Democratic seizure. Both sides were armed but the Black defenders proved no match against the white attackers' numbers and armaments. Waving white flags, the black defenders surrendered, but were nevertheless mowed down after laying down their weapons. An estimated 153 Black men were killed. Far from a mere dispute over an election, one of the attack's leaders made the aim clear: "Boys, this is a struggle for white supremacy."

Propensity for Violence

Wilmington Insurrection November 10th, 1898

Before the violence started, black voters were a numerical majority in Wilmington, NC. By the end, they were a minority. In local elections two days before the violent coup d'état, biracial coalitions elected a white Republican mayor and a biracial city council while white Democrats won the rest of the state. Furious at the election results in Wilmington, a white supremacist and former Confederate, Alfred Moore Waddell, led 2,000 insurrectionists against the city's legitimately elected officials, attacked Black homes and businesses, and installed himself as mayor.

Red Summer May 1st, 1970

As America demobilized from World War I, whites frustrated by job and housing shortages rioted in over three dozen cities during the summer of 1919, killing hundreds and injuring thousands of African Americans.

Propensity for Violence

White mobs initiated every attack, but the press blamed Bolshevist agitation while others faulted the "attitude" of returning Black soldiers.

Tulsa Race Riot May 31st thru June 1st, 1921

For 14 hours in 1921, mass violence engulfed Tulsa, OK. White rioters killed around.
Three hundred black Tulsans, injured hundreds, and leveled the black section of town—
Greenwood. The riot began after thousands gathered to lynch a Black teen suspected of assaulting a white teen. When a small contingent of armed Black men tried to prevent the lynching, the white mob began looting and shooting wildly as rumors of a "Negro uprising" spread.

The police and hastily deputized recruits rounded up thousands of black Tulsans into detention centers while white vigilantes set Greenwood ablaze— even using planes to bomb the area.

Ku Klux Klan Kon Klave August 9th, 1963

In 1925, 30,000 Klan members marched down Pennsylvania Avenue in Washington, D.C. Klan membership soared in the 1920s after the release of *Birth of a Nation* (1915) and amid immigration fears. Expanding its hate to Jews and Catholics, the 1920s Klan held a more prominent and national role than its earlier iteration. In marches like this, its brand of nativism, bigotry, intimidation, and extralegal violence were shrouded in patriotism. Women and children attended the march too, giving the event a picnic atmosphere.

Propensity for Violence

16th Street Baptist Church Bombing September 15th, 1963.

Two weeks after Martin Luther King Jr.'s "I Have a Dream" speech, Klan members bombed an Alabama church with two hundred worshipers inside. Killing four children and injuring twenty-two others, the bomb was the fourth in Birmingham in as many weeks in a city nicknamed **"Bombingham."** Fed up, Black residents protested that night, but were met only with violence.

Greensboro Massacre November 3, 1979

A 1979 anti-Klan rally in Greensboro, NC turned violent when forty members of the Klan and American Nazi Party arrived with guns and fired into the crowd after the anti-Klan protestors pelted their vehicles with rocks. Klansmen killed five and wounded a dozen others.

for the Klan to be "beaten and chased out of town" as "this is the only language they understand," but were unprepared for the ensuing violence. Despite being filmed by a local TV news crew, the 5 Klansmen charged with murder were acquitted by an all-white jury with the claim of self-defense. In 2009, the Greensboro City Council passed a resolution.

Overland Park Jewish Community Center Shooting April 13th, 2014.

Klan members and other hate groups have long disparaged Jewish Americans, but the
2014 shooting at a Jewish community center in Kansas by an elderly former Army Green Beret, Klansman, and neo-Nazi shocked the nation. Frazier Glenn Miller killed three people, including a 14-year-old boy, to kill as many Jews

as he could. Miller failed, however, as his three victims were Christians. Miller had a long history of anti-Semitism, insisting that white people needed protection from Jews. Unlike many other white supremacist killings, Miller received a death sentence for his crimes. Upon conviction, he yelled "Sieg Heil" and gave the Nazi salute. So, these are a few horrible incidents in American History but as they say, "The Victor writes the history books." So those who write said books dictate what is written and what is omitted. The omitted portions tell and do not tell what the facts are. With certain thing inserted i.e., who was the villain, who was the hero, who was the victims, who are the savages. The African was seen by Western Culture as the violent savage as well as the Native Americans. Once you stand back and accurately look at what has been going one its scary. I've sat in thought and I keep hearing in this day and age about a coming race war. Well let me be the first to say that we are in a race war as we speak and I never really knew it. Not a Cold War but a current one. The original colonist arrived here, in the Americas, started a race war with the original Native Americans. Then they invaded Africa and took prisoners of war, i.e., African Slaves and made to work in Labor Camps. And the race war with Mexicans. The race war is not coming the race war is here and now.

Propensity for Violence

Seeing and reading about what has been going on since the 1900's to now, it almost gives one the feeling of an atmosphere of Black Genocide and or a Genocide of any race that the Western Culture is inferior to them. The forced enslavement of Africans, but not just the enslavement but the shear brutality and treatment of any races of color. The racial hate in this Western Culture is so thick you can cut it with a knife, with hate comes violence towards those for whom they have hate. Violence to the point where you beat that race to submission. If their resolve still holds, they are killed. The raping of not only woman but the male slaves as well-known as Buck Breaking. This was done publicly in front of the other males slaves to keep them in check. The constant degradation of any race of color.

The Violence of Religion in White Supremacy

Jonathan Riley-Smith writes,

The consensus among Christians on the use of violence has changed radically since the crusades were fought. The just war theory prevailing for most of the last two centuries—that violence is an evil which can in certain situations be condoned as the lesser of evils—is relatively young. Although it has inherited some elements (the criteria of legitimate authority, just cause, right intention) from the older war theory that first evolved around A.D. 400, it has rejected two premises that underpinned all medieval just wars, including crusades: first, that violence could be employed on behalf of Christ's intentions for mankind and could even be directly authorized by him; and second, that it was a morally neutral force which drew whatever ethical coloring it had from the intentions of the perpetrators.

Manifest destiny is the belief that it was Americans' mission to expand from the east coast of North America all the way to the west coast. American settlers would settle throughout this area and, over time, set up many settlements. The land that they were settling on included Texas, California, Oregon, and New Mexico.

The underlying concept of Manifest Destiny came from the belief in the 19th century that the United States had the God-given right to expand its territories across the entire continent. The population swelled from 5 million people in 1800 to more than 23 million just five decades later.

Violence and racism are also written in the Christian Bible. The same Bible that is used currently and then by Western Culture. In the days of slavery, the Christian Bible was one of the few books' slaves were allowed to read. I'm sure one of the reasons is that the Christian Bible contained passages that taught slaves to obey their master's so says the Lord. Slave owners where concerned the bible verses would incite their Slaves to rebel. But they soon realized that portions of the bible had scriptures containing submission to authority, so the Christian slave owners created the **Slave Bible** which was made from selected parts to inspire submission. White Christians felt this version, which was created in 1807 by unknown authors, was needed for the conversion of slaves. Now, during the birth of Christianity there were many things that were done in the name of God and religion. Kings and Clerics killed and conquered in the name of God. Kings would invoke war, cross over a mountain and kill, burn, and pillage because God told them to do so. I'm to kill your first born, because God told me to do so. I'm going to take your daughters and make them our wives and your elders our slaves because God told me to do so. The whole idea of a hierarchy of the human race was developed throughout the sixteenth century by Anglo-Saxon Protestants who used religion to justify the enslavement of Africans. Religious leaders were the main ones at the forefront supporting Jim Crow Laws, Segregation, and Anti-Miscegenation Laws. White Mobs would plan lynchings on Sunday afternoons where the entire town would participate on the front lawns of black churches to instill fear in their congregation.

The Bible

(King James Version)

"Tell slaves to be submissive to their masters and to give satisfaction in every respect; they are not to talk back, not to pilfer, but to show complete and perfect fidelity, so that in everything they may be an ornament to the doctrine of God our Savior. (Titus 2:9-10) Slaves, accept the authority of your masters with all deference, not only those who are kind and gentle but also those who are harsh. For it is a credit to you if, being aware of God, you endure pain while suffering unjustly. If you endure when you are beaten for doing wrong, what credit is that? But if you endure when you do right and suffer for it, you have God's approval. (1 Peter 2:18-29)"

One of the many religious leaders supported slavery to a great degree also using his religion believes to justified having slaves. One of these believers was the Rev. Robert Lewis Dabney in his book *A Defense of Virginia* he writes about providence and God's will of Africans being ruled by the Superior Race.

Rev. Robert Lewis Daney

"Was it nothing, that this race, morally inferior, should be brought into close relations to a nobler race, so that the propensity to imitation should be stimulated by constant and intimate observation, by domestic affection, by the powerful sentiment of allegiance and dependence?".

As defined in Wikipedia:

Christian Identity (also known as **Identity Christianity**) is an interpretation of Christianity which advocates the belief that only Celtic and Germanic peoples, such as the Anglo-Saxon, Nordic nations, or Aryan people and people of kindred blood, are the descendants of Abraham, Isaac, and Jacob and are therefore the descendants of the ancient Israelites. Independently practiced by individuals, independent congregations, and some prison gangs, it is not an organized religion, nor is it affiliated with specific Christian denominations. Its theology is a racial interpretation of Christianity. Christian Identity beliefs began to develop in the early 1900s among adherents of British Israelism by authors who regarded Europeans as the "chosen people" and regarded Jews and non-whites as the cursed offspring of Cain, who they believed was a "serpent hybrid". This aspect of Christian Identity theology is commonly called the serpent seed or two-seedling doctrine. White supremacist sects and gangs later adopted many of these teachings.

Christian Identity promotes the idea that all non-whites (people who are not of wholly European descent) will either
be exterminated or enslaved in order to serve the white race in the new Heavenly Kingdom on Earth under the reign of Jesus Christ. Its doctrine states that only "Adamic" (white) people can achieve salvation and enter paradise. Many of its adherents are Millennialist. It is considered racist, antisemitic, and white supremacist by
the Anti-Defamation League and the Southern Poverty Law Center. As of 2014, estimates of the number of adherents in the United States range from two thousand to fifty thousand. By the second half of the 20th century The Christian Identity Movement proclaimed being the direct descendants from the biblical tries of Israel and that Armageddon is the ultimate battle of white against the non-whites hence the white supremacy even in religion.

A need to be Superior.

British writer, Rudyard Kipling, in 1899 wrote "The White man's Burden, to bring civilization to Non-White peoples through beneficent imperialism. So, Rudyard Kipling felt as though it was a burden that White Men had to brig Non-Whites to civilization. That God rested all of that on their shoulders. So, the question I have is are you superior or do you feel insecure? Are you superior to every other race on the planet or do you really feel intimidate by other races?

What makes a Person Act superior to another person?
"When a person acts superior to another, they really feel
that the other is a perceived threat. In some way they
believe others will find out that they really are 'inadequate'
and therefore behave in ways that make them feel like they
are 'better' than the rest."

What Is a Superiority Complex?

A superiority complex is a behavior that suggests a person believes they are somehow superior to others. People with this complex often have exaggerated opinions of themselves. They may believe their abilities and achievements surpass those of others. However, a superiority complex may be hiding low self-esteem or a sense of inferiority. Psychologist Alfred Adler first described the superiority complex in his early 20th century work. He outlined that the complex is really a defense mechanism for feelings of inadequacy that we all struggle with. In short, people with a superiority complex frequently have boastful attitudes to people around them. But these are merely a way to cover up feelings of failure or shortcoming.

How to tell if you have a superiority complex
The symptoms of superiority complex may include:

- high valuations of self-worth

- boastful claims that are not backed up by reality.

- attention to appearance, or vanity.

- overly high opinion of oneself

- a self-image of supremacy or authority

- unwillingness to listen to others.

- overcompensation for specific elements of life

- mood swings, often made worse by contradiction from another person.

- underlying low self-esteem or feelings of inferiority

You may believe that you spot some of these symptoms in another person. They can be easy to identify, especially after a long relationship. But matching these symptoms to the complex itself is not that easy. Many of these "symptoms" can also be caused by several other conditions. These include narcissistic personality disorder and bipolar disorder.

A Psychological Causes of Violence

The most common motivations for violence can be viewed as inappropriate attempts to manage emotions. Often, violence is the medium used by an individual to openly express their feelings such as anger, frustration, or sadness. Other times, violence can be considered as a form of manipulation for individuals to try and get what they want or need. Aggressive behavior can also be used as a form of retaliation; a means by which one uses to even the score. Finally, violent behavior is sometimes caused because people grow up seeing violence openly displayed. Violence then becomes learned as an "appropriate" way to behave.

Narcissism and Violence

Is it possible to be too self-centered? Are there consequences of unchecked bragging? According to a new study from The Ohio State University, the answer is yes. Researchers say narcissism can lead to aggression and violence. The researchers analyzed over 430 studies from around the world and found that narcissism is an important risk factor for both aggression and violence. They identified the link for all degrees of narcissism, from just a few traits to full blown narcissistic personality disorder (NPD), regardless of gender, age, or country of residence. "It's disturbing to know that there is such a consistent link between being high in the trait of narcissism because it doesn't have to be at pathological levels, and being high in aggression," **Sophie Kjærvik, MA,** a doctoral student at Ohio State and study author, tells Very well. Anywhere between 1% to 17% of the

United States population may have NPD. But this study's results apply even to those who don't develop the disorder. Nearly everyone has some degree of narcissism, Kjærvik adds, which makes its links to aggression and violence important to study.

Narcissistic personality disorder:

One of several types of personality disorders is a mental condition in which people have an inflated sense of their own importance, a deep need for excessive attention and admiration, troubled relationships, and a lack of empathy for others. But behind this mask of extreme confidence lies a fragile self-esteem that's vulnerable to the slightest criticism. A narcissistic personality disorder causes problems in many areas of life, such as relationships, work, school, or financial affairs. People with narcissistic personality disorder may be generally unhappy and disappointed when they're not given the special favors or admiration, they believe they deserve. They may find their relationships unfulfilling, and others may not enjoy being around them.

Propensity for Violence

I believe, from my readings. That Anglo-Saxon Protestants could be suffering from narcissistic personality disorder (NPD). These people have a need for admiration and have lack of empathy for others. Patterns of Narcissistic abusive patterns are as follows:

1) An Inflated sense of self
2) Preoccupation with power or success
3) Sense of entitlement and expectation of special treatment.
4) The need to control and exploit others.

People with this condition if that is what you want to call it. Tend to be violent and or abusive. Another technique used by Narcissist is **Gaslighting.**

Gas Lighting

Psychological manipulation of a person usually over an extended period of time that causes the victim to question the validity of their own thoughts, perception of reality, or memories and typically leads to confusion, loss of confidence and self-esteem, uncertainty of one's emotional or mental stability, and a dependency on the perpetrator. *Gas Lighting* can be a highly effective tool for the abuser to control an individual. It's done slowly so the victim writes off the event as a one off or oddity and doesn't realize they are being controlled and manipulated.—

Narcissistic try to control what you think and say and threaten to punish you if you disobey. Another is a lack of boundaries. Signs of abuse are lack of boundaries of those who insert themselves i.e., Karen's, who violate your sense of privacy. Verbal abuse is another form of narcissism.

Effects on Victims:

1) Shame
2) Anxiety
3) Guilt
4) Fearing Powerless
5) Confusion
6) Loss of self-esteem

Symptoms

Signs and symptoms of narcissistic personality disorder and the severity of symptoms vary.

People with the disorder can:

- Have an exaggerated sense of self-importance.

- Have a sense of entitlement and require constant, excessive admiration.

- Expect to be recognized as superior even without achievements that warrant it.

- Exaggerate achievements and talents.

- Be preoccupied with fantasies about success, power, brilliance, beauty, or the perfect mate.

- Believe they are superior and can only associate with equally special people.

- Monopolize conversations and belittle or look down on people they perceive as inferior.

- Expect special favors and unquestioning compliance with their expectations.

- Take advantage of others to get what they want.

- Have an inability or unwillingness to recognize the needs and feelings others.

- Be envious of others and believe others envy them.

- Behave in an arrogant or haughty manner, coming across as conceited, boastful, and pretentious

- Insist on having the best of everything — for instance, the best car or office

At the same time, people with narcissistic personality disorder have trouble handling anything they perceive as criticism, and they can:

- Become impatient or angry when they don't receive special treatment

- Have significant interpersonal problems and easily feel slighted.

- React with rage or contempt and try to belittle the other person to make themselves appear superior.

- Have difficulty regulating emotions and behavior.

- Experience major problems dealing with stress and adapting to change.

- Feel depressed and moody because they fall short of perfection.

- Have secret feelings of insecurity, shame, vulnerability, and humiliation.

Sadistic Personality Disorder

Sadistic personality disorder was a personality disorder defined by a pervasive pattern of sadistic and cruel behavior. People with this disorder were thought to have desired to control others. It was believed they accomplish this by physical or emotional violence. This diagnosis appeared in an appendix of the *Diagnostic and Statistical Manual of Mental Disorders* (DSM-III-R).[1] The later versions of the DSM (DSM-IV, DSM-IV-TR, and DSM-5) do not include it. It was removed as psychiatrists believed it would be used to legally excuse sadistic behavior.

Symptoms and behaviors

Sadistic personality disorder was defined by a pervasive pattern ego-syntonic of sadistic behavior. Individuals possessing sadistic personalities tend to display recurrent aggression and cruel behavior.[2][3][4] People with this disorder will use violence and aggression in an attempt to control and dominate others. When others refuse to submit to their will, they will increase the level of violence they use. Many sadists will verbally and emotionally abuse others rather than physically, purposefully manipulating others through the use of fear or shaming and humiliating others. Some people with this disorder will not abuse others, but will instead display a preoccupation with violence.[5][6] This disorder was thought to be caused by childhood trauma or being raised in by a family where one spouse is abused. Sadistic personality disorder was considered more common in men than women.

Comorbidity with other personality disorders Sadistic personality disorder was thought to have been frequently comorbid with other personality disorders, primarily other types of psychopathological disorders.[5] In contrast, sadism has also been found in patients who do not display any or other forms of psychopathic disorders.[8] Conduct disorder in childhood, and Alcohol use disorder were thought to have been frequently comorbid with Sadistic personality disorder.[5][9] Researchers had difficulty distinguishing sadistic personality disorder from the other personality disorders due to its high levels of comorbidity with other disorders.[5]

Diagnostic criteria

According to the DSM-III-R diagnostic criteria Sadistic personality disorder is defined by a pervasive pattern of sadistic and cruel behavior that begins in early adulthood. It was defined by four of the following.

Propensity for Violence

- Has used physical cruelty or violence for the purpose of establishing dominance in a relationship (not merely to achieve some non-interpersonal goal, such as striking someone in order to rob him/her).
- Humiliates or demeans people in the presence of others.
- Has treated or disciplined someone under his/her control unusually harshly.
- Is amused by, or takes pleasure in, the psychological or physical suffering of others (including animals).
- Has lied for the purpose of harming or inflicting pain on others (not merely to achieve some other goal).
- Gets other people to do what he/she wants by frightening them (through intimidation or even terror).

- Restricts the autonomy of people with whom he or she has a close relationship, e.g., will not let spouse leave the house unaccompanied
- or permit teenage daughter to attend social functions.
- Is fascinated by violence, weapons, injury, or torture.

Propensity for Violence

And again, after you've read this section, there is from what I see in the symptoms are the same personality and behavior of Anglo-Saxon Protestant. From slavery to now. The use of cruelty and violence against slaves and African Americans during Jim Crow. The humiliation and demeaning of African Americans with the label "Nigger" which to me is not just a word for blacks but to make African Americans feel dirty and less than a human being. One of the greatest fears any human being does not what to ever and misery on all who cross their path. Native Americans African Americans Woman Children even their own they call **"White Trash."**

The behavior is horrible, but the icing on the cake is the ability they have to find and tap into the fear of their victims. How they humiliated and eradicated the Native American. How they beat and subjugated Africans with in public display. How they kept the woman in fear through domestic violence and or fear of rape.

How vulnerable children living in constant fear of physical and sexual abuse. Then their own who they consider whom are even below them even though they are the same race. Always the need to dominate over something or someone.

A Propensity for Violence

The United Nations (UN) Defines genocide as any of the following acts committed with intent to destroy, in whole or in part, a national, ethnical, racial, or religious group, as such: Killing members of the group; Causing serious bodily or mental harm to members of the group. The United States Code, in Section 1091 of Title 18, defines genocide as violent attacks with the specific intent to destroy, in whole or in part, a national, ethnic, racial, or religious group, a definition like the Convention on the Prevention and Punishment of the Crime of Genocide.

Propensity for Violence

In 1965 Malcolm X was assassinated while engaged in efforts to prosecute the United States Government before the United Nations and the World Court for its complicity in the existence of a genocidal situation for Black Americans based on the UN's own definition of genocide.

Propensity for Violence

On April 3, 1964, Malcolm X delivered one of his most famous speeches, "The Ballot or the Bullet," in which he elaborated on his earlier statements." First, Malcolm X believed the struggle needed to be expanded from civil rights to human rights to remove the issue from the domestic jurisdiction of the United States.3 Second, he explained that the Negro problem had never been brought to the United Nations because a conspiracy existed within the United States. 4 Malcolm X elaborated: "the old, tricky, blue-eyed liberal ... keep you wrapped up in civil rights. And you spend so much time barking up the civil-rights tree, you don't even know there's a human rights-tree on the same floor. 35 Third, he revealed his ideological conception of human rights as natural rights applicable on a universal basis. He stated: "human rights are something you were born with. Human rights are your God-given rights.

Human rights are the rights that are recognized by all nations of this earth. And any time anyone violates your human rights, you can take them to the world court. '36 Finally, Malcolm X felt that if the struggle was internationalized, Africa, Asia, and Latin America would all throw their weight behind the struggle.37

Thus, Malcolm X's liberating paradigm centered upon his intention to utilize the United Nations as a Pan-African forum to illustrate the international human rights violations perpetrated by the United States upon its citizens of color.

Propensity for Violence

Violence is the leading cause of death in the United States. Western Culture has committed everything from massacres to genocides. The United States have come the master's at killing. It's gone from Bow and Arrows to Nuclear Weapons. Others country export cars, clothing, wine, and electronics. The only thing that the United States produces and exports is Viagra and Weapons. There is the NRA and the US Constitution both guarantying the ability to keep, use, and bear arms. There are moments where Anglo-Saxon Protestant are quick to resort to some degree a violence. The point that I'm making in this book, after standing back a looking at Western Culture behavior and I might sound stupid but I feel like there is something seriously wrong with this Culture, at every turn they are so quick to resort to violence to some degree. From what was done to Slaves to Indians.

Propensity for Violence

Violent episode after violent episode and it made me wonder if they had a serious mental condition. I am saying this to be facetious. But what little I know about mental illness there seems to be a correlation between violence and Anglo-Saxon Protestant. No other culture behaves like this.

White fragility triggers

Racial stressors may cause a range of defensive behaviors and emotions. White people may act in certain ways when people of color discuss racism.

Their reactions may include:

- anger
- fear
- guilt
- arguing
- silence
- leaving the stress-inducing situation

Propensity for Violence

I think that once you sum this all together it just comes down to this. Anglo-Saxon Protestants live in fear. This fear had been there from the beginning but not as intense. In the beginning, during slavery the fear was subtle. White slave owners, even though they were into control. Feared the slave and felt the need to chain them like animals. They projected their primal emotions onto the African, so to chain us physically is a chain them mentally. But at the end of the day Anglo-Saxons fears the muscularity and size of the Black male. That is why there were story after story of Black slaves being castrated by the white slave masters, meaning that there was some degree of penis envy or jealousy of the Black man. They felt sexually threaten by the black man being gifted physically and sexually. This also brought on the sexual desires of the white woman. So, of there must be some kind of connection between fear and violence among white people. Fear that is so great it causes them to lash out physically to hurt or killed the one they fear the most. So, after slavery the fear started to grow.

Black men starting to own land, and homes. Starting to raise families. The fear grew because now the white man started to realize that eventually this Nigger is going to become my equal. This point is brought home no stronger than the incident in Tulsa "Black Wall Street" Of 1921. In the Greenwood District of Tulsa was the area where the black culture flourished. Black families owning home, Blacks owning businesses, blacks owning banks, poor whites coming to these black banks to get loans.

Once word got out regarding the goings on in Greenwood, a dark cloud storm that storm was a storm crated with fear and hate the one could ever image existed. The hate and rage was so great it was though the Devil himself came to Tulsa and burned it to the grown. And when that storm passed Greenwood was no more.

Propensity for Violence

So as time went on both emotions of the white culture fed each other as African American culture grew. The fear fed the rage and in turn the rage fed the fear. The fear of how Malcom X, with one phone call could summon thousands of Muslim Men to any point and time, And they were quoted as saying:

"No one man should have that much power',

quotes a police officer's response to a pivotal Harlem protest that Malcolm X organized. That fear the Malcom X could call all black men to rally and fight the white establishment. While this was going on, inter racial dating was also on the rise. Yes the Nigger Loving white women where dating and marring black men, and the result from this is inter racial children.

White would result in the gene pool of the white culture to start to diminish from the pure white nation. As time went on the fear of how black men would rise in sports, in the corporate world, in politics. There has always been and always will be fear of the black race. There are facts that cause this to occur in Anglo-Saxons.

Revenge

The enslavement of Africans resulted in a plethora of uprisings, from the Haitian Rebellion to Nat Turner's rebellion. Since then, whites have developed a pathological fear that oppressed Blacks will one day rise up and inflict vengeance upon their oppressors.

Projection

The psychological defense mechanism called projection – when one accuses someone of having traits they refuse to acknowledge in themselves – may also explain why white people fear violence from Black people. Instead of acknowledging the past and present forms of violence Black people have suffered at the hands of whites, it is projected onto the victims themselves.

Media Propaganda

Historically and up until present times, the media continue to broadcast daily imagery of Black men as dangerously criminal, using and dealing drugs, hypersexual, unemployable, and idle and the epitome of death and doom. This is true despite the reality that white people have, and do, participate in mob and domestic violence in higher numbers, and that whites comprise more than 70 percent of drug abusers and dealers in our country.

Moral Blindness

White people's fear of Blacks also stems from a form of moral blindness, in which Black bodies remind them of the terrible crimes from an ugly past, but they are unable to own up to it because they have bought into the Black predator myth and practice projection. Instead, they deny, shift blame, lie, twist facts and characterize Black people into a people to fear.

Reprisal from Fellow Whites

Whites also fear becoming outcasts among whites by associating and sympathizing with Black folks.

Genetic Annihilation

Dr. Frances Cress Welsing, author of *The Isis Papers*, argues that because whiteness is genetically recessive, some whites fear that integration and miscegenation will result in the annihilation of the white race. Therefore, they established a global system of "White Supremacy" and its subsystems of racism and segregation to prevent it.

Fear of Black Power

Many whites who directly benefit from the current plight of Black people fear that their enlightenment and subsequent organizing will result in the inability to exploit and benefit from their resources, as well as a reclaiming of their historic legacy.

Propensity for Violence

I genuinely believe that the cause and effect of White Supremacy and the treatment of people of other colors. It is because that 1, you're afraid that if given the chance African Americans they would do the same things to white Americans that was done to them and 2 the fear because of their own insecurity mentally and physically. And 3, look and check into what I have been writing in this book. I do believe that the white Western Culture is suffering from a deep mental illness. Now I am not saying this to let them off the hook but to try to help it make scene. The next time your at work, or out and about, or watching something on the news, just pause a watch the white male. Peel back the cover and see the inter mentally ill person inside. We are dealing with those who know nothing but fear and violence. The fear they have on races of color, and the violence they bring upon them. So yes the United States of America for years has had nothing but **a Propensity for Violence.**

www.ingramcontent.com/pod-product-compliance
Lightning Source LLC
Chambersburg PA
CBHW061445040426
42450CB00007B/1219